This book Expertly Colored by ....

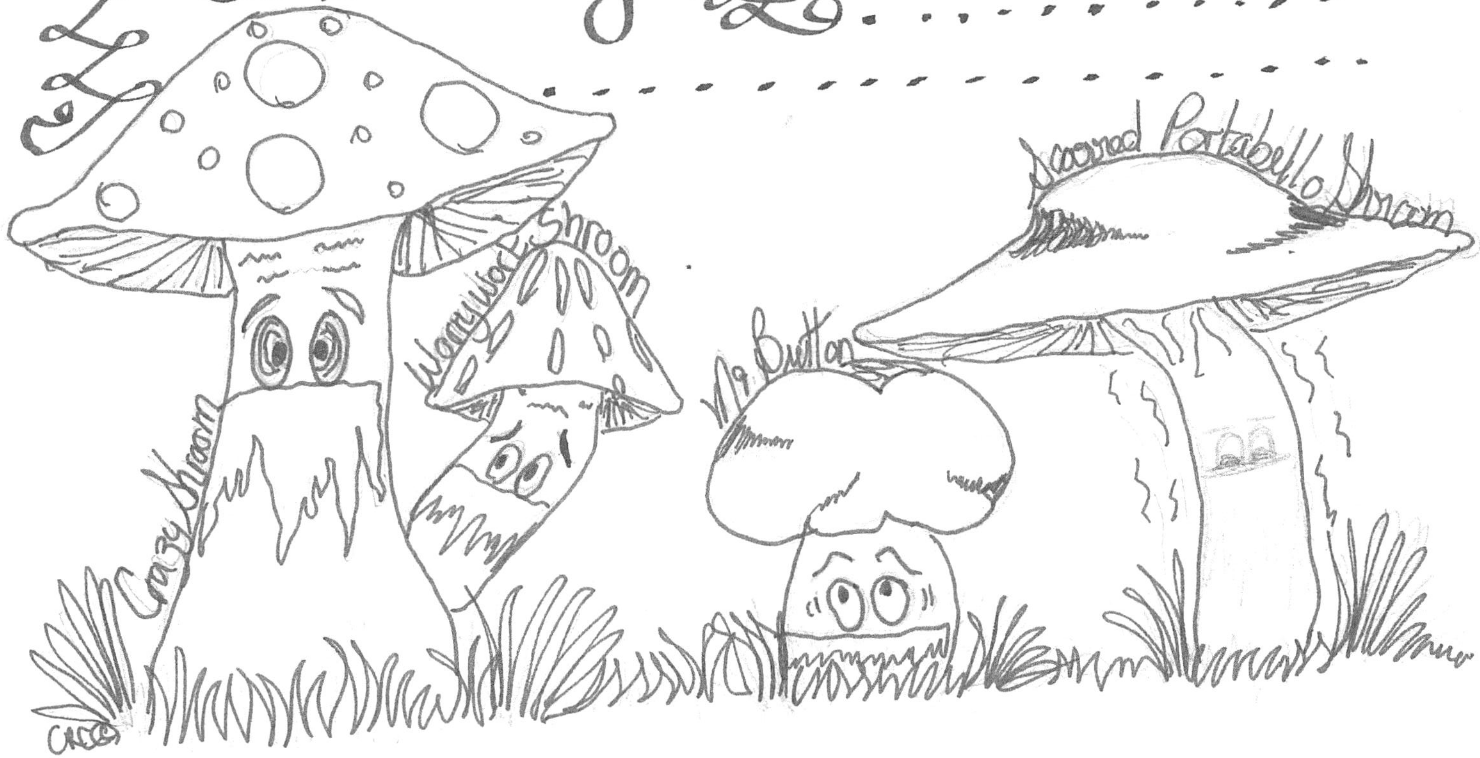

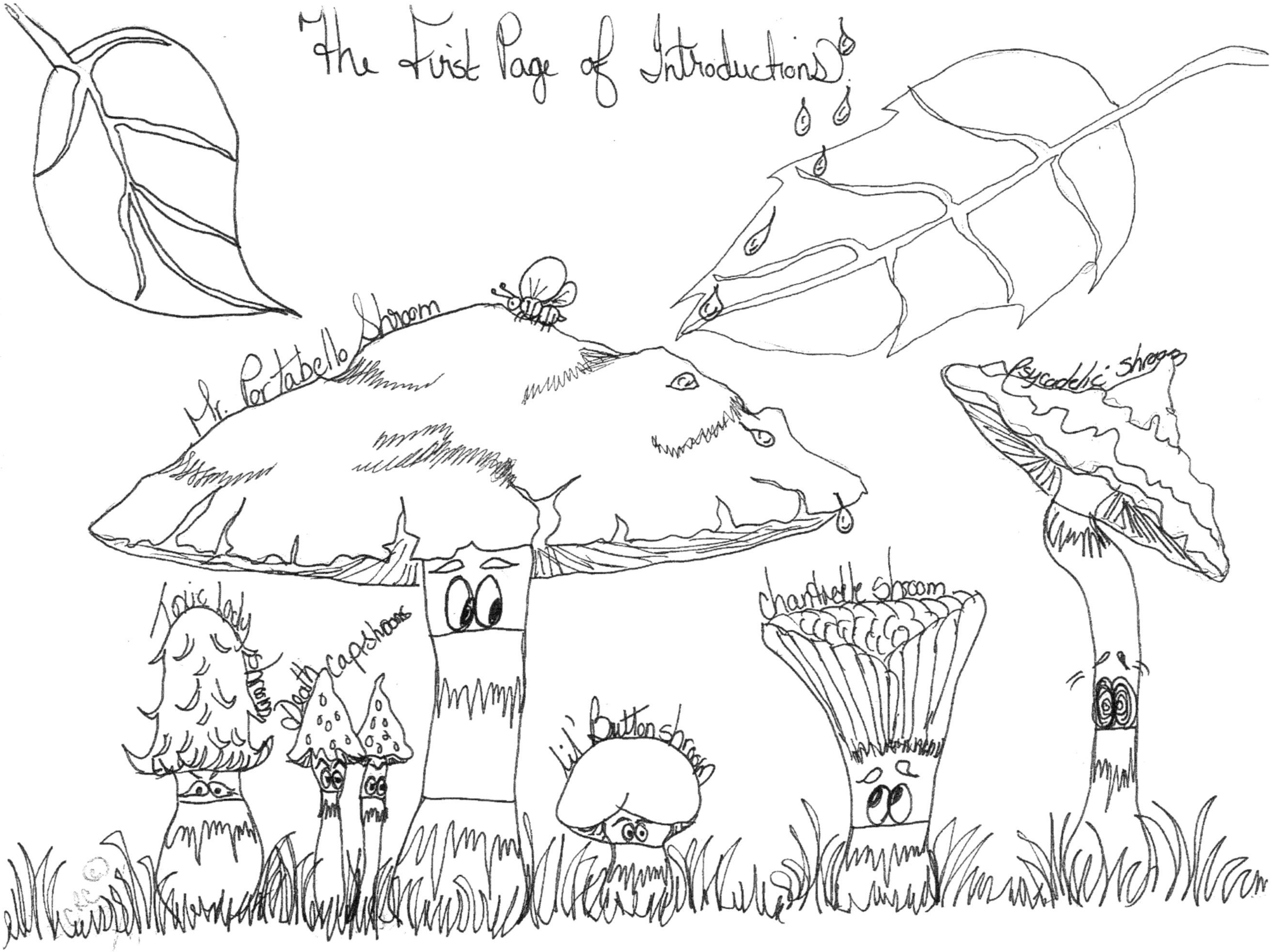
The First Page of Introductions
Mr. Portabello Shroom
Psycadelic shroom
Toxic lady shroom
Death capshrooms
Lil' Buttonshroom
chanthelle shroom

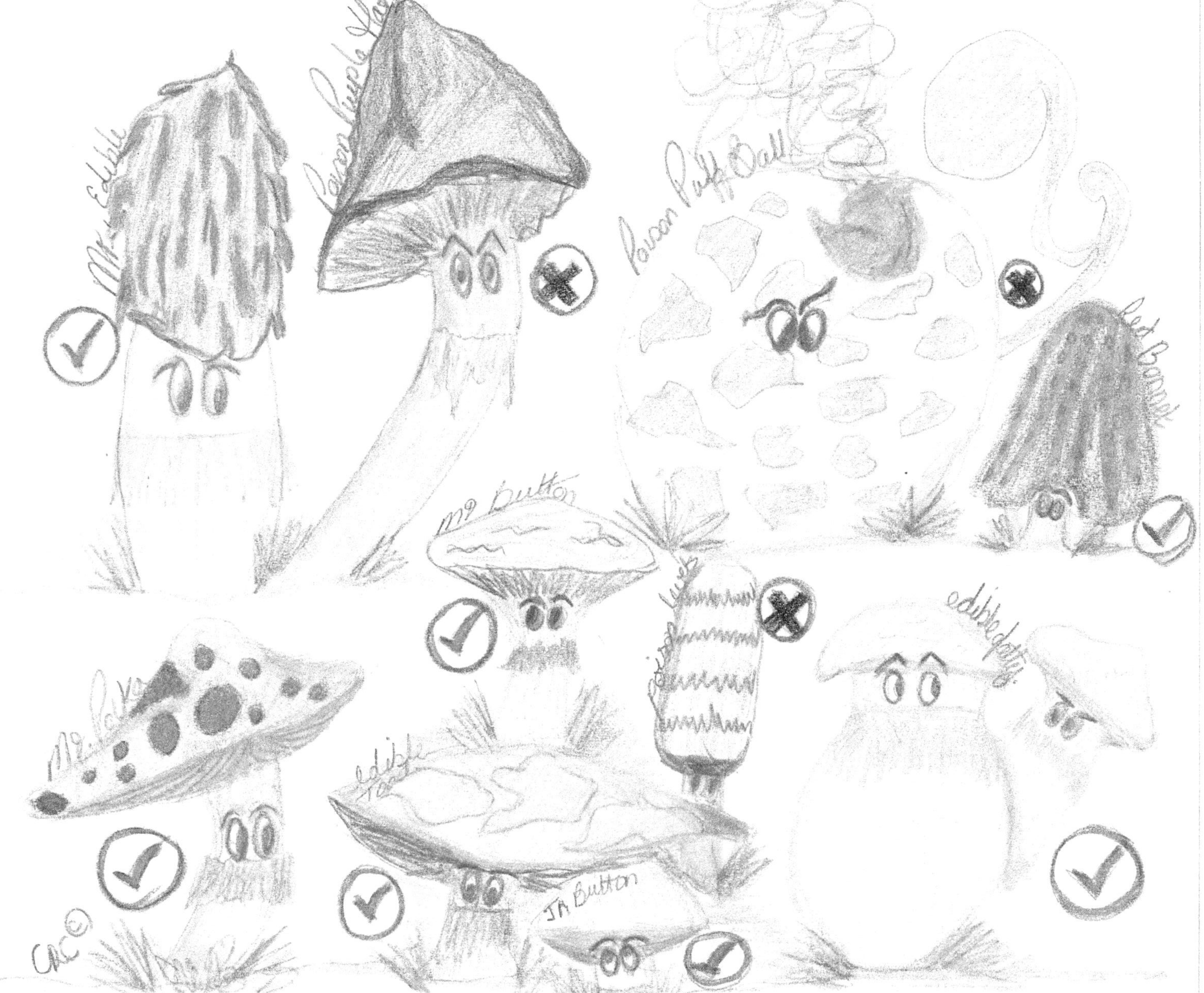

Mr. Edible
Poison Puff Ball
Red Bonnet
Mr Button
edible dotty
JR Button
CAC©

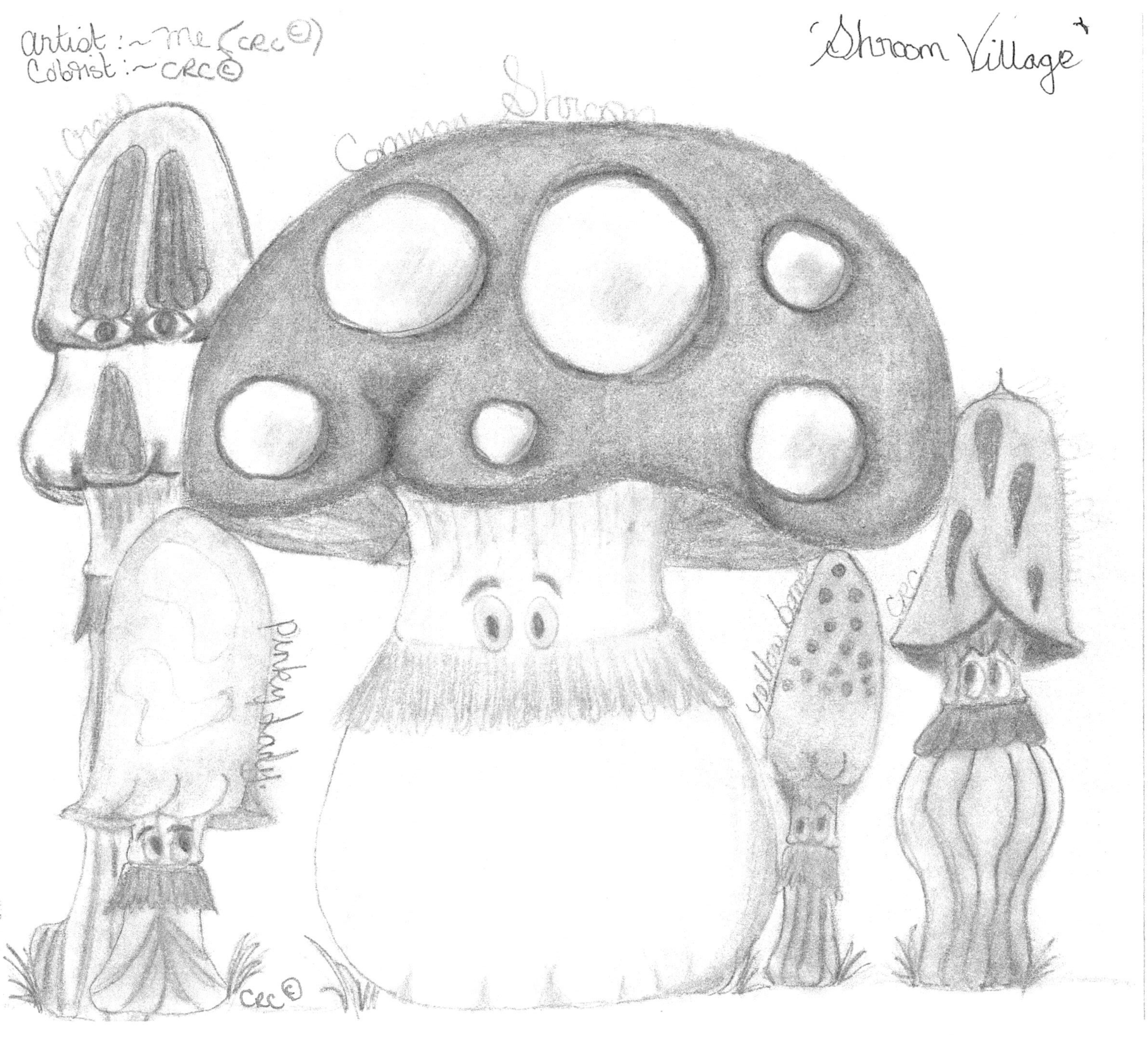
'Shroom Village'
Artist: ~ me (CRC©)
Colorist: ~ CRC©
Common Shroom
pinky lady.
CRC©

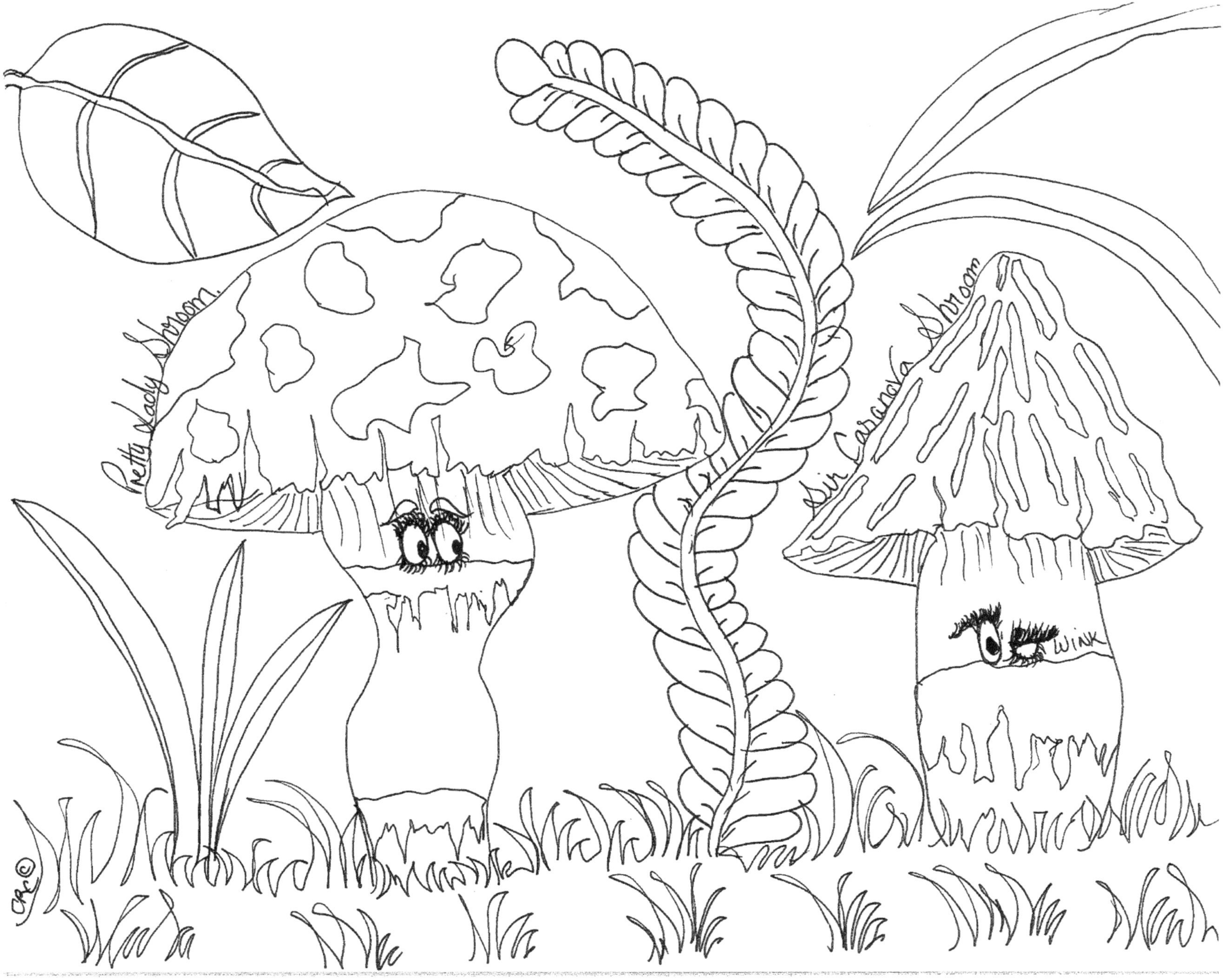
Pretty Lady Shroom.
Sir Casanova Shroom
WINK
CPC©

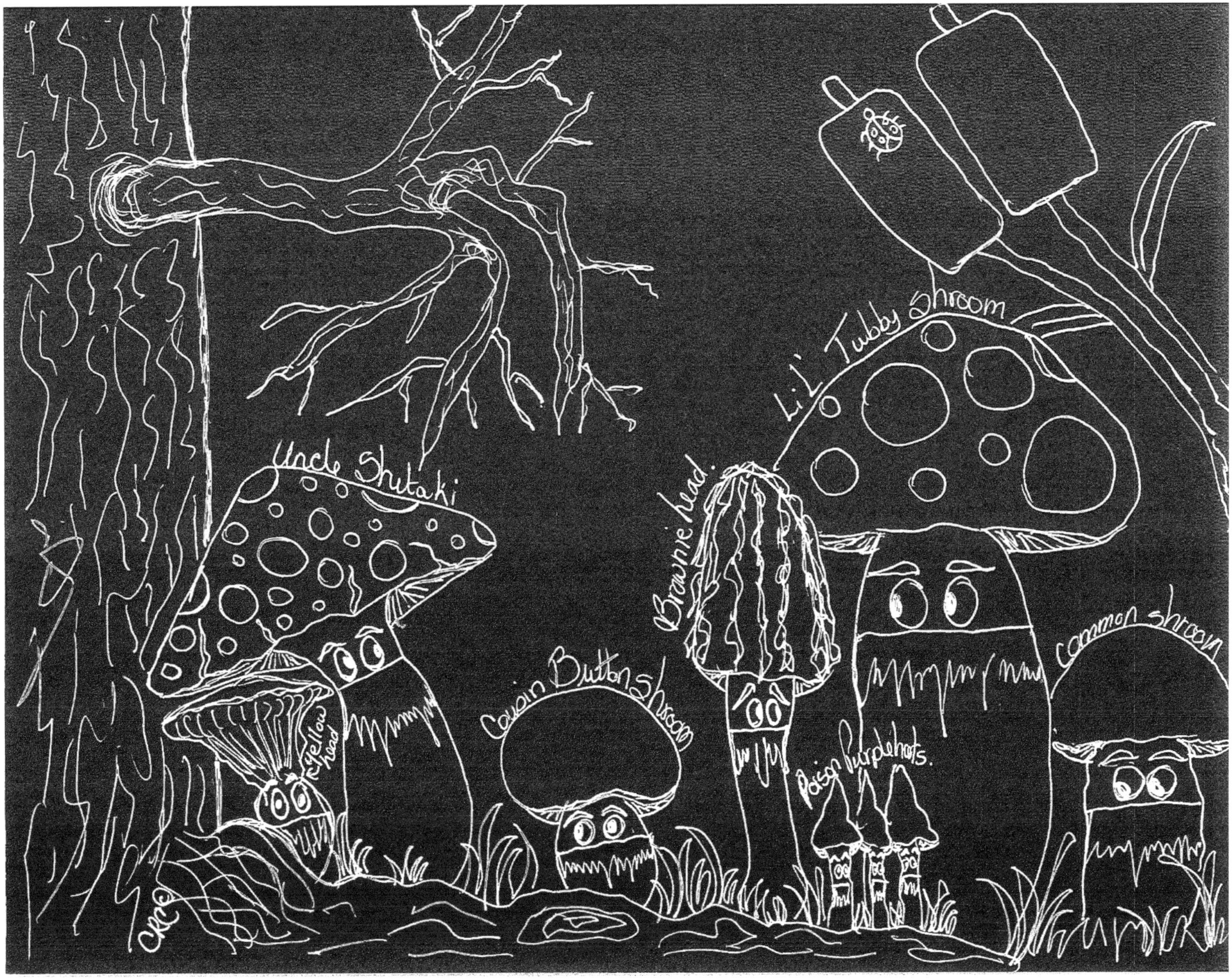

Uncle Shitaki
Yellow head
Cousin Buttonshroom
Brownie head.
Li'L' Tubby shroom
Poison Purplehats.
common shroom
CRC©

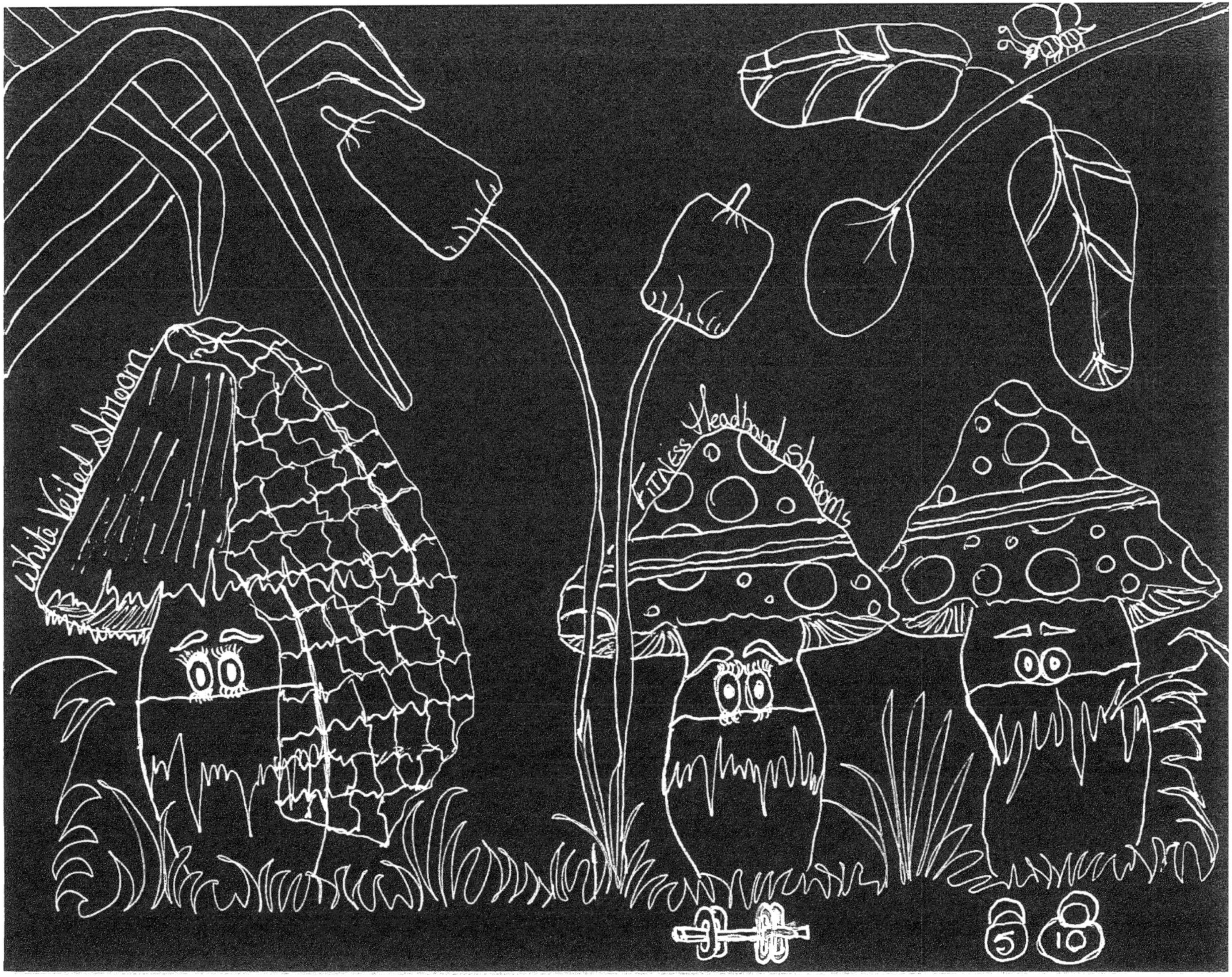
White Veiled Shroom
Fitness Headband Shrooms
5
10

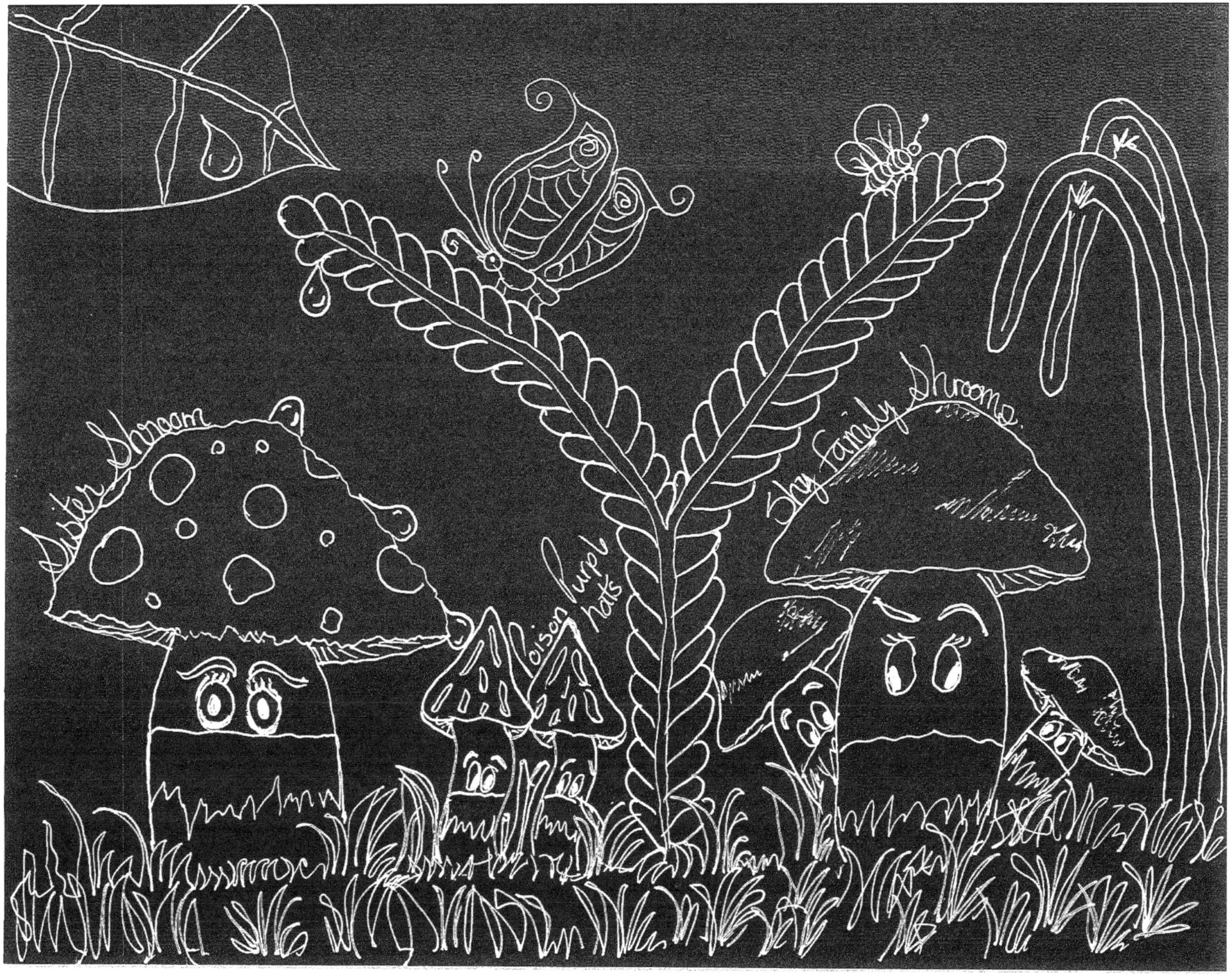
Sister Shroom
Poison Purple hats
Shy family Shrooms

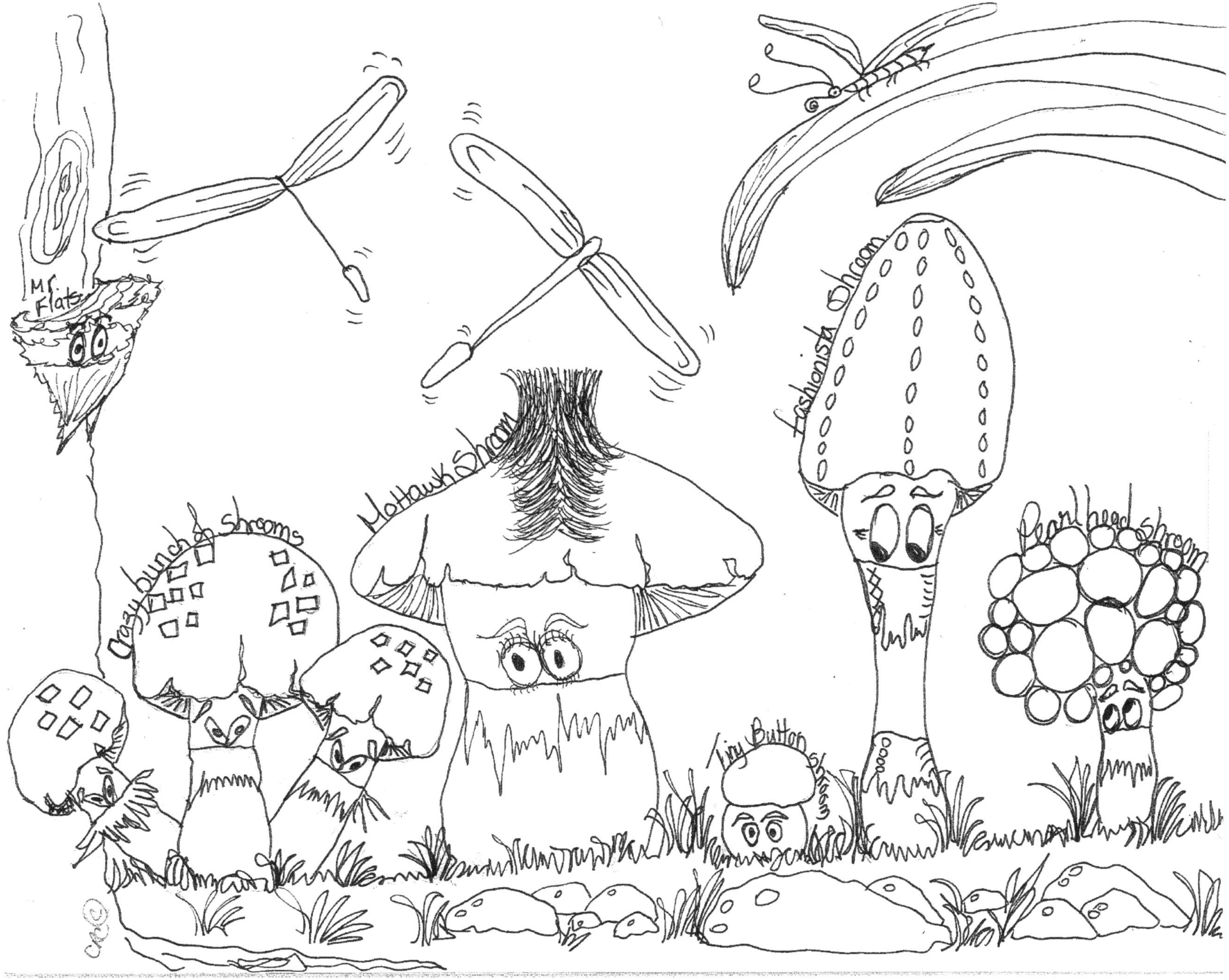
Mr. Flats
Crazy bunch of shrooms
Mohawk Shroom
Fashionista Shroom
Pearlhead shroom
Tiny Button shroom

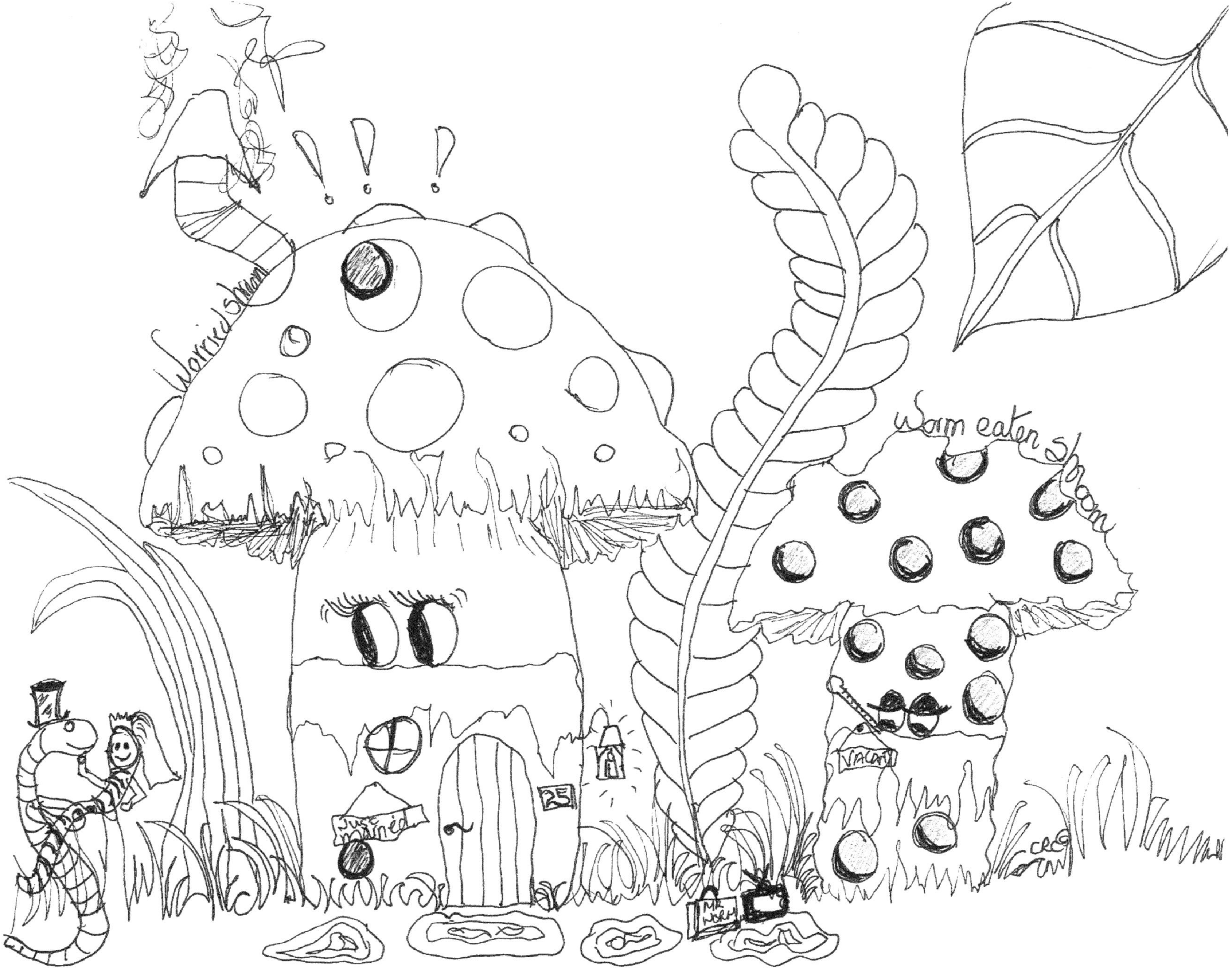

Worried shroom
Worm eaten shroom
Just married
25
VACANT
MR WORM

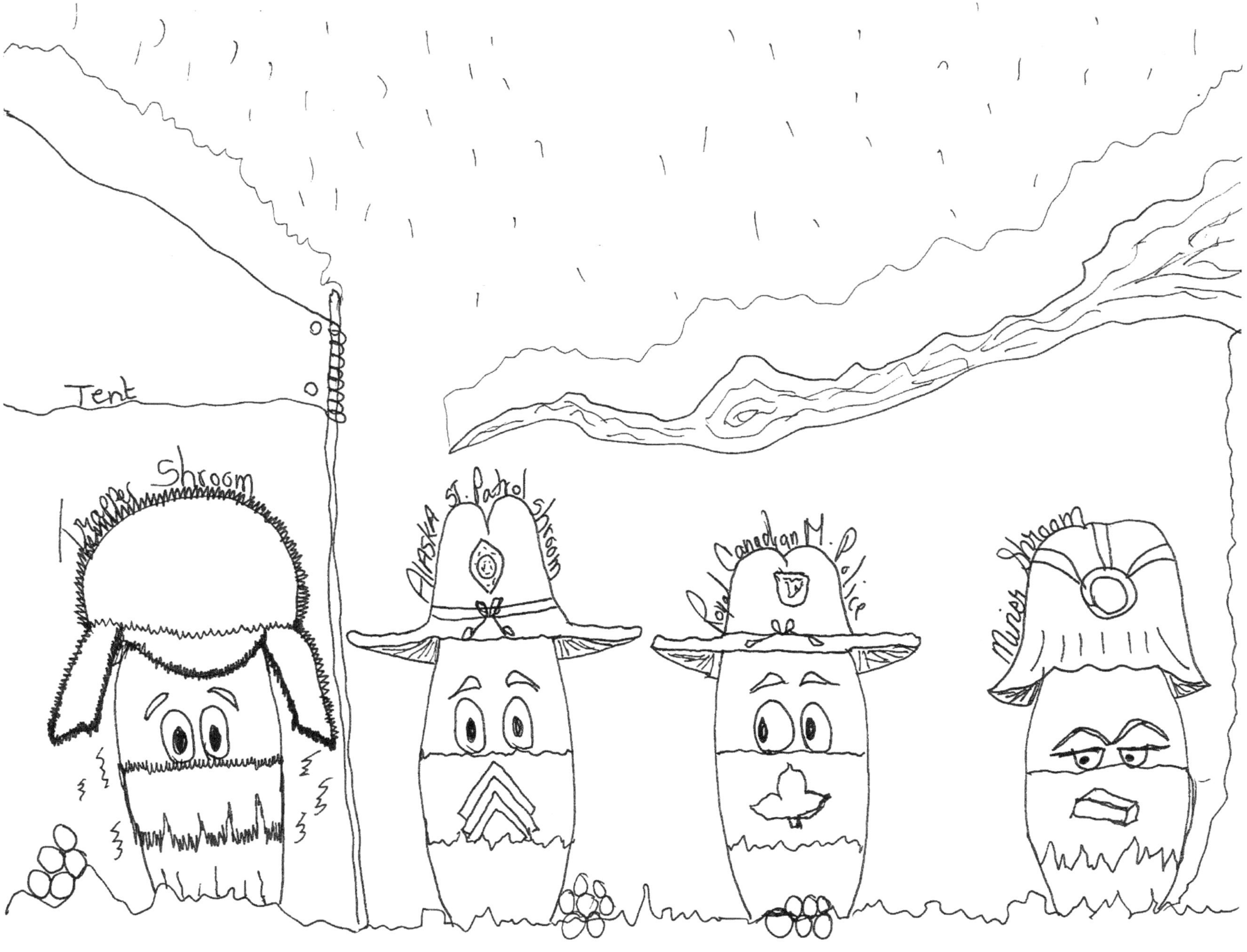
Tent
Trapper Shroom
Alaska St. Patrol Shroom
Royal Canadian M. Police
Miner Shroom

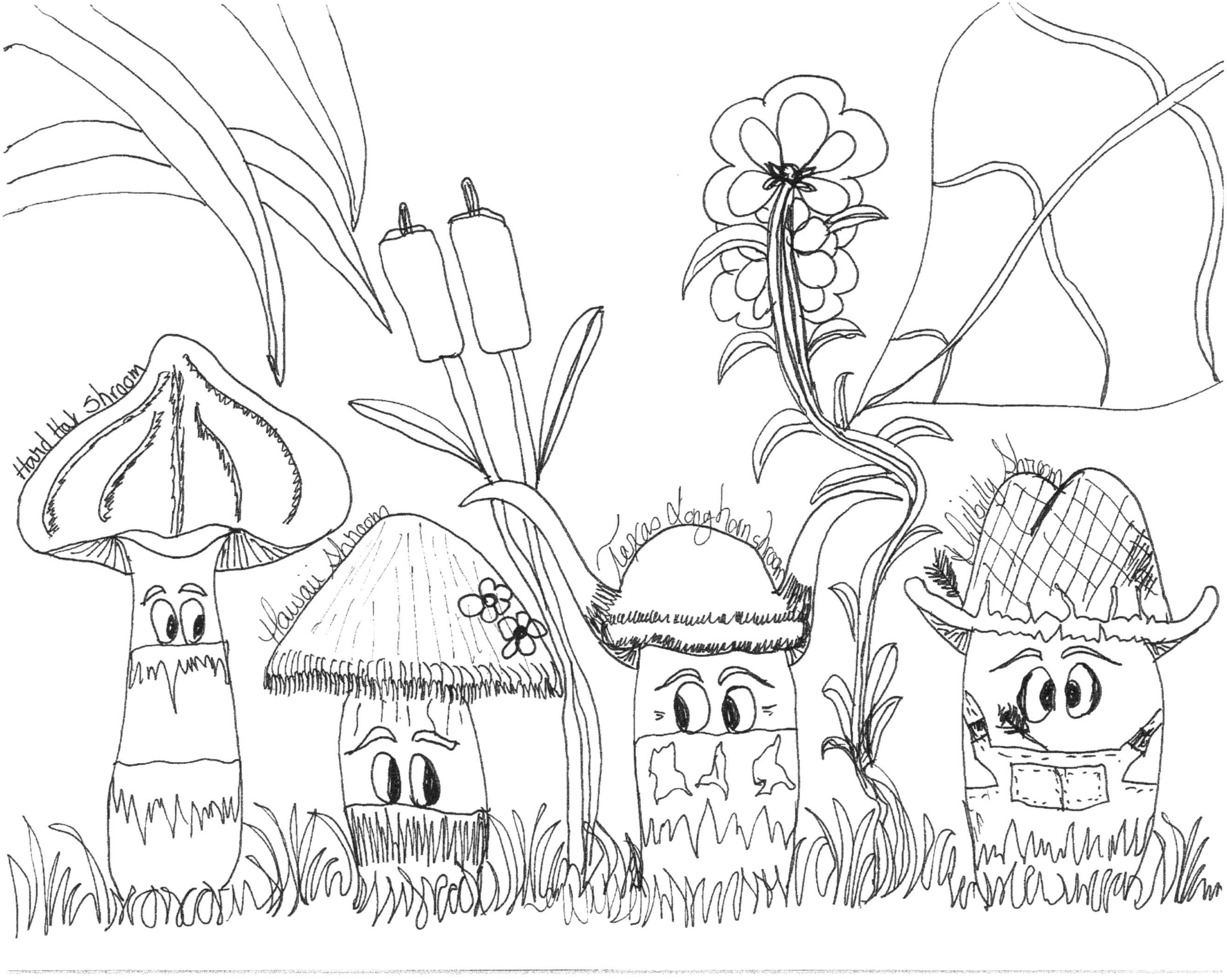

Hard Hat Shroom
Hawaii Shroom
Texas Longhorn Shroom
Hillbilly Shroom

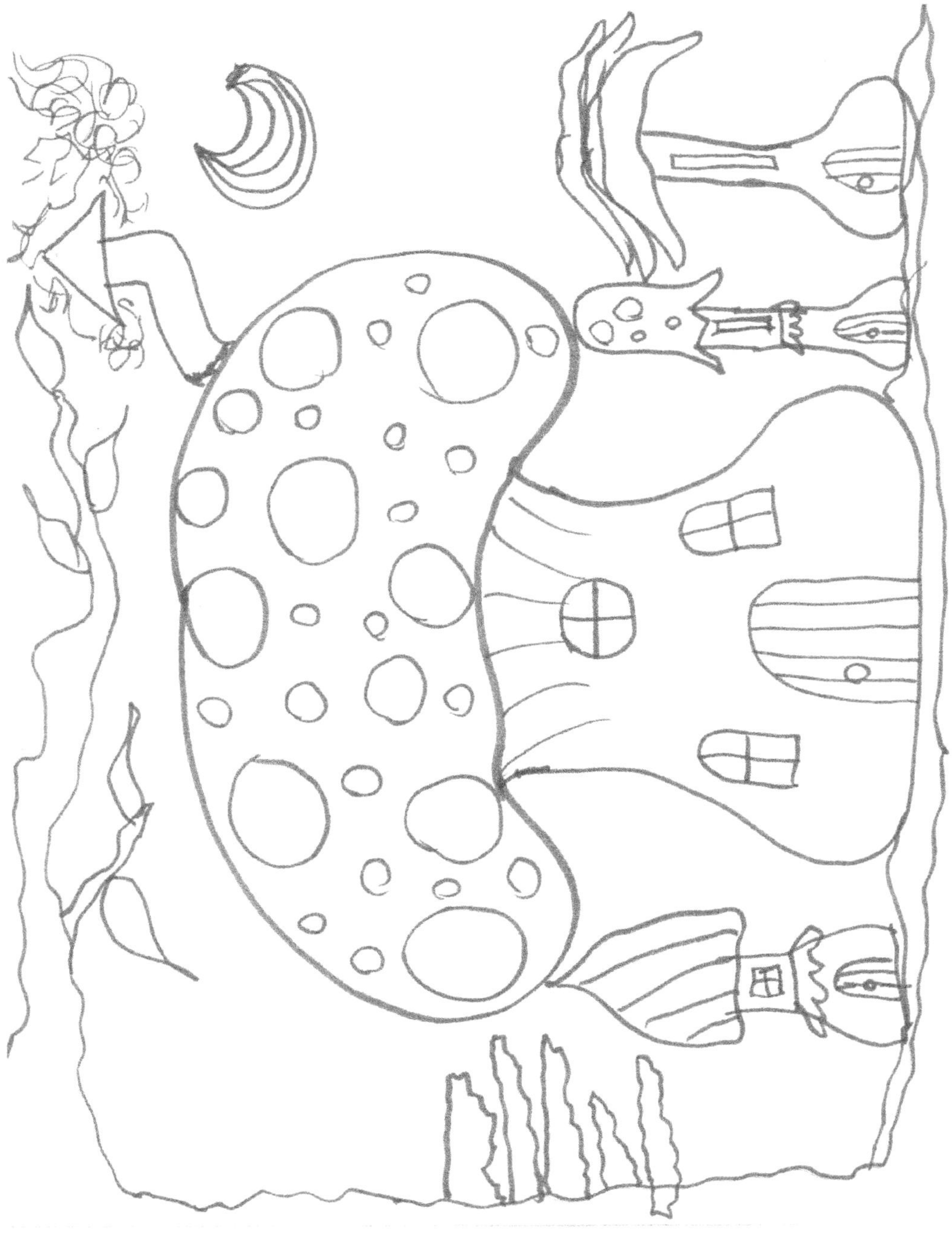

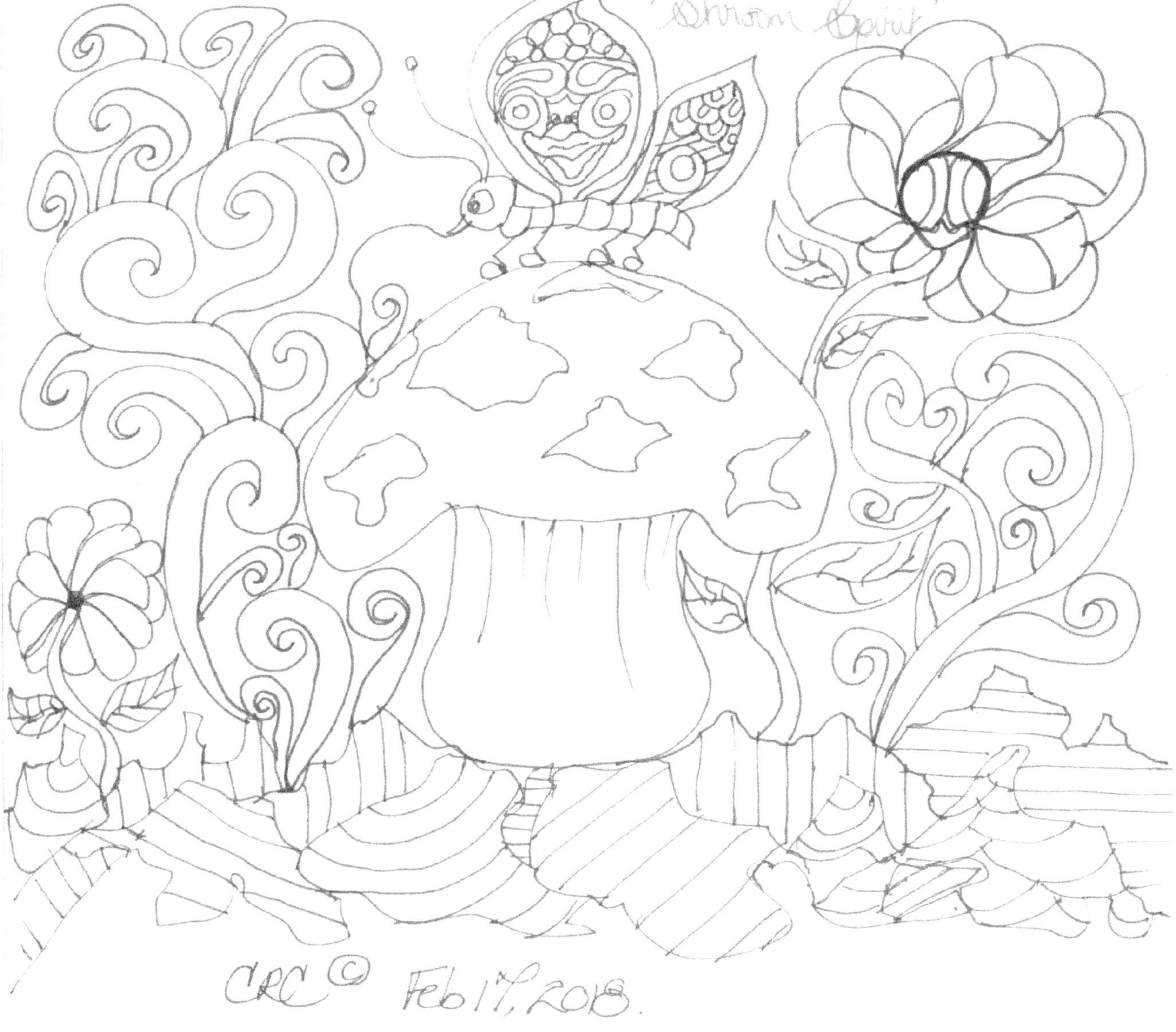
'Shroom Spirit'
CRC © Feb 17, 2018.

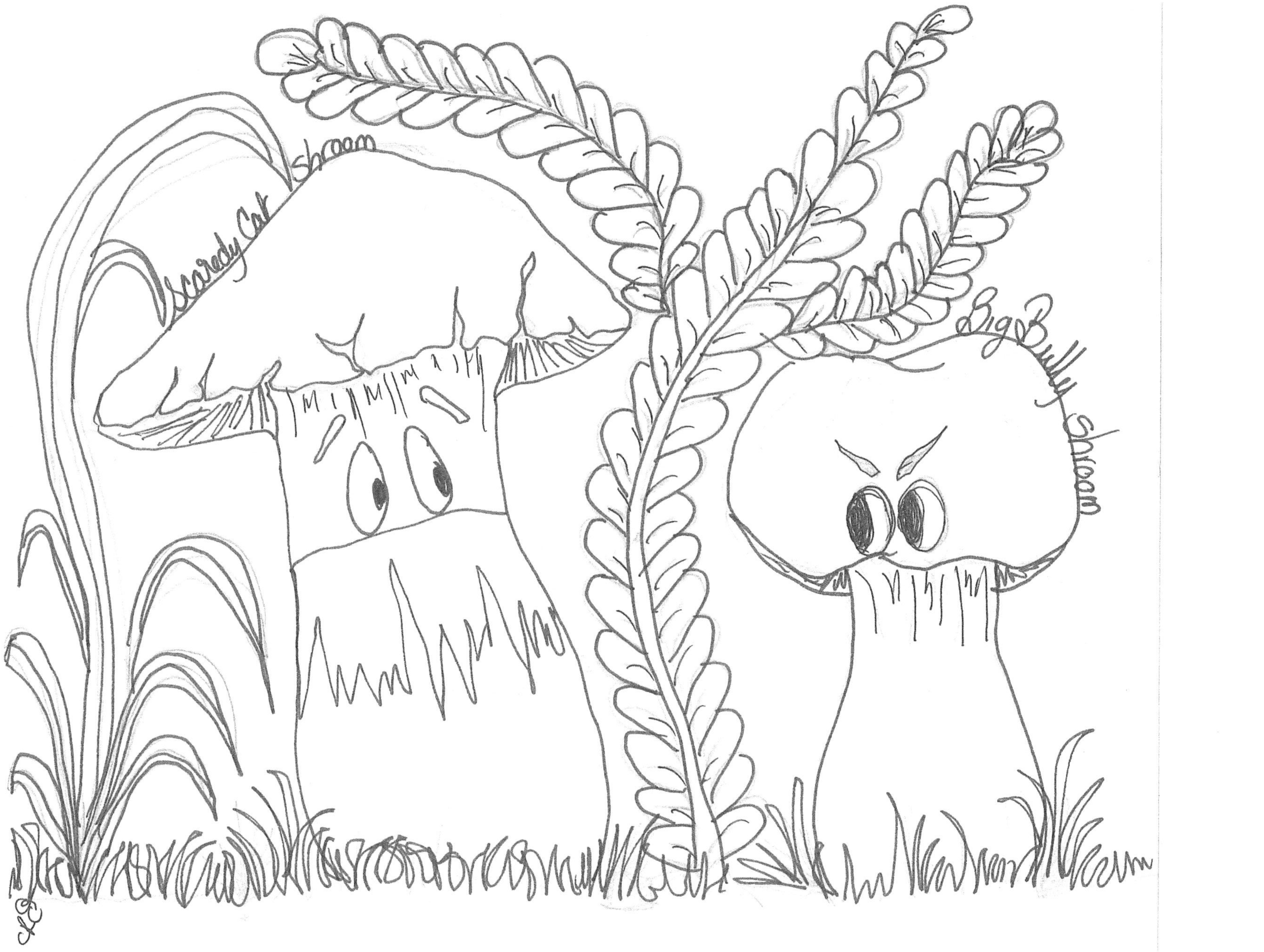
Scaredy Cat shroom
Big Bully shroom

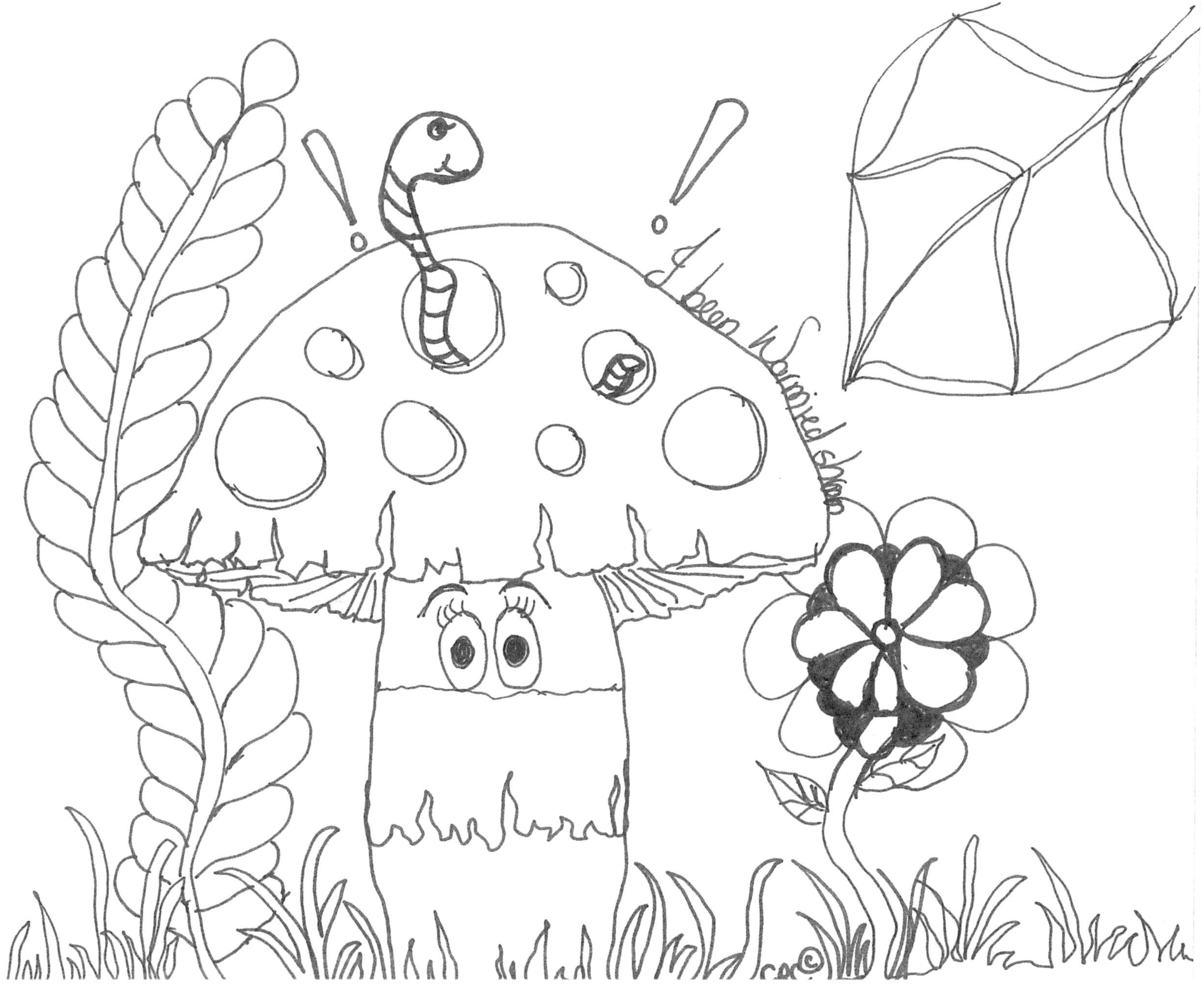
I been Wormied shroom

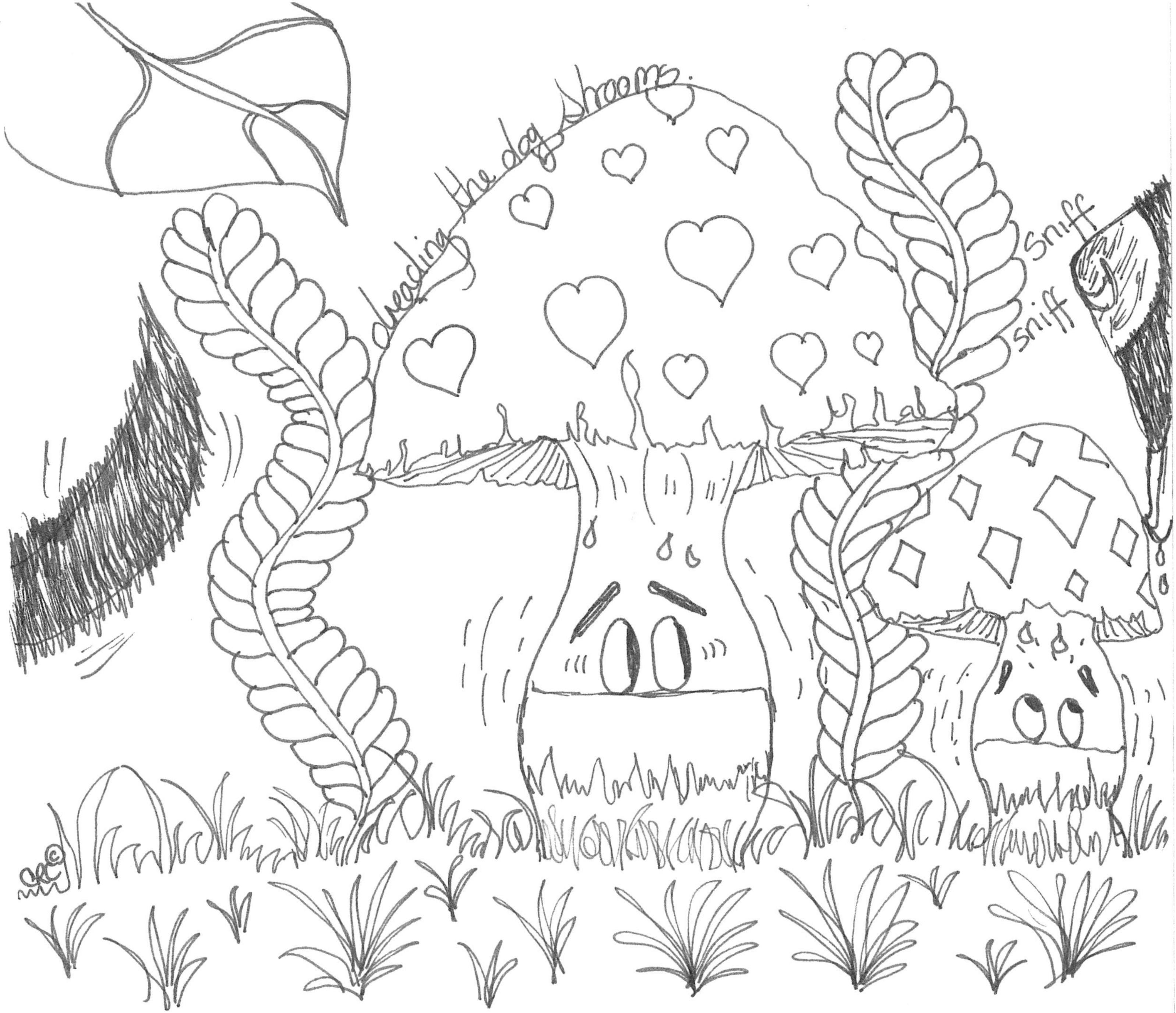
dreading the dog. Shrooms.
Sniff
sniff

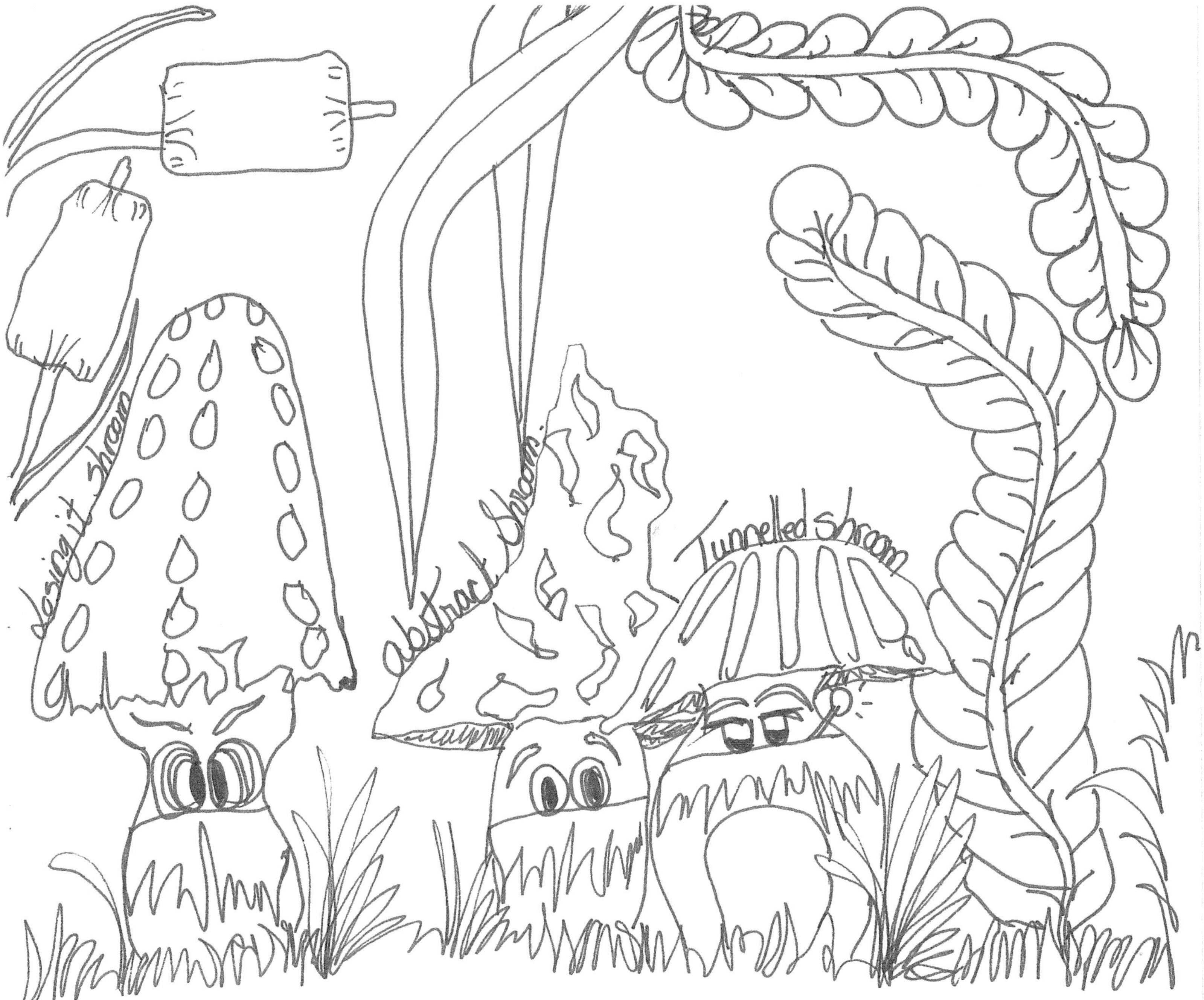
losing it shroom
abstract Shroom
Tunnelled shroom

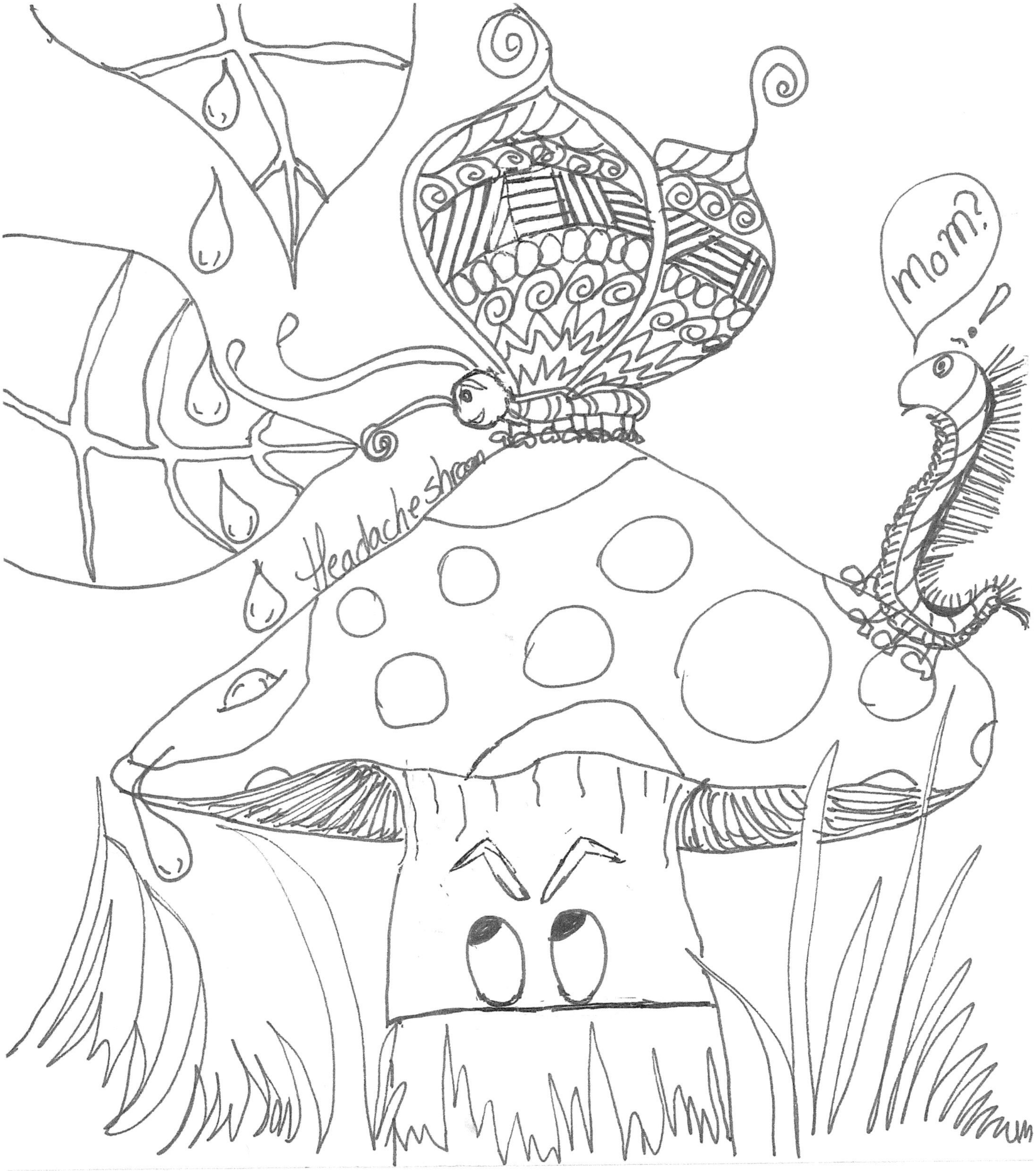
mom?
Headacheshroom

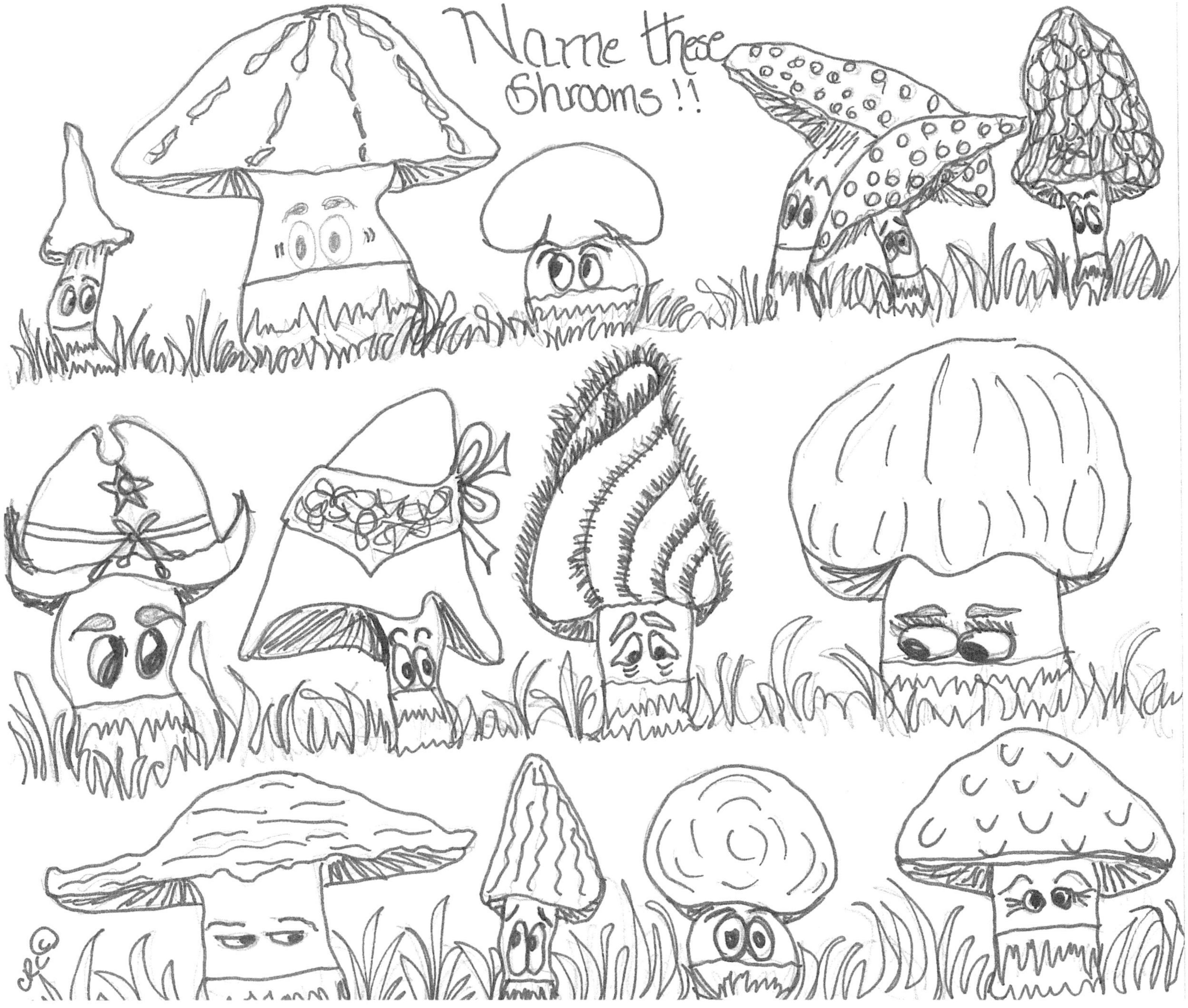
Name these Shrooms!!

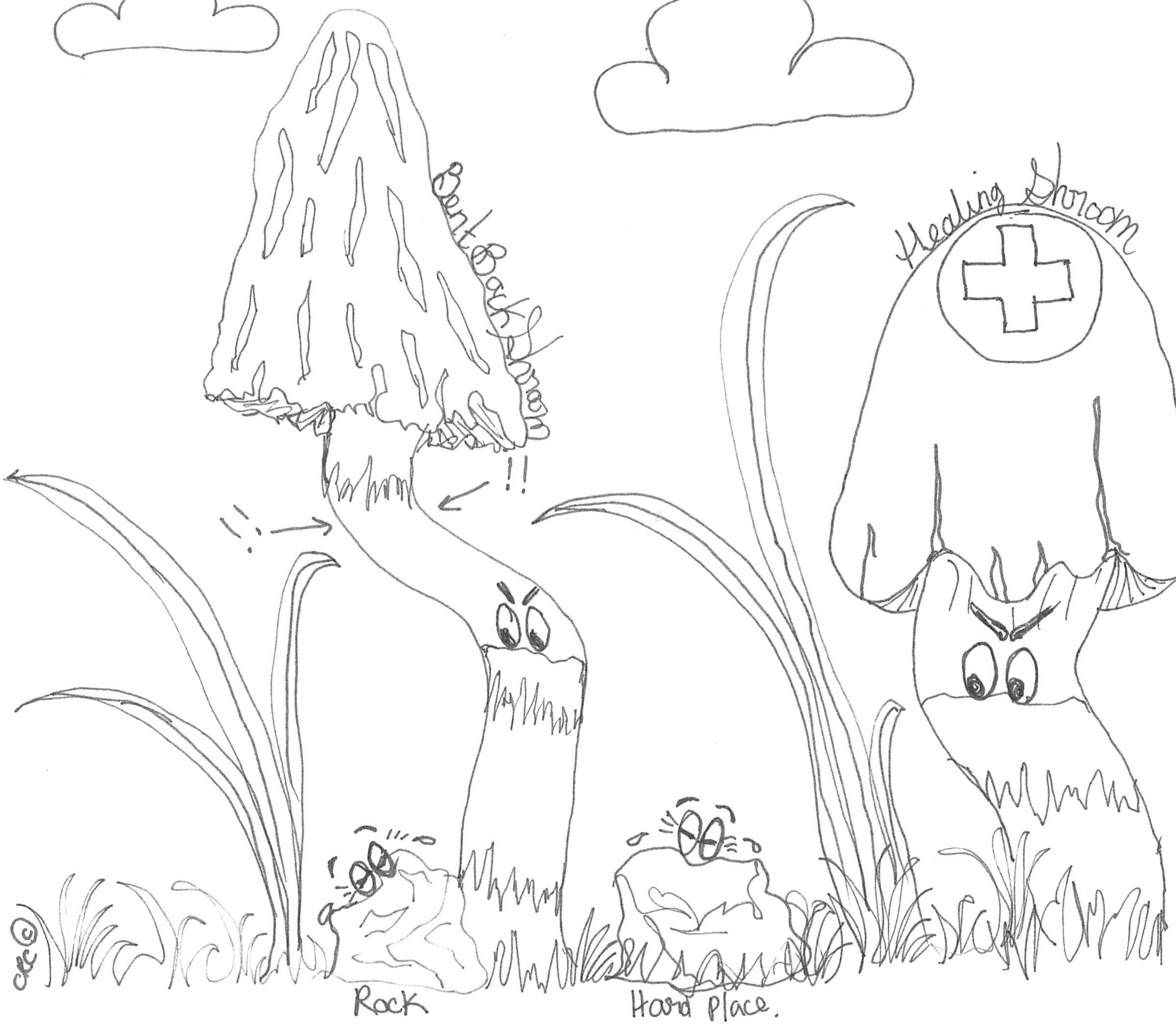
Bent Back Shroom
!!
!!
Healing Shroom
Rock
Hard place.
©CRC

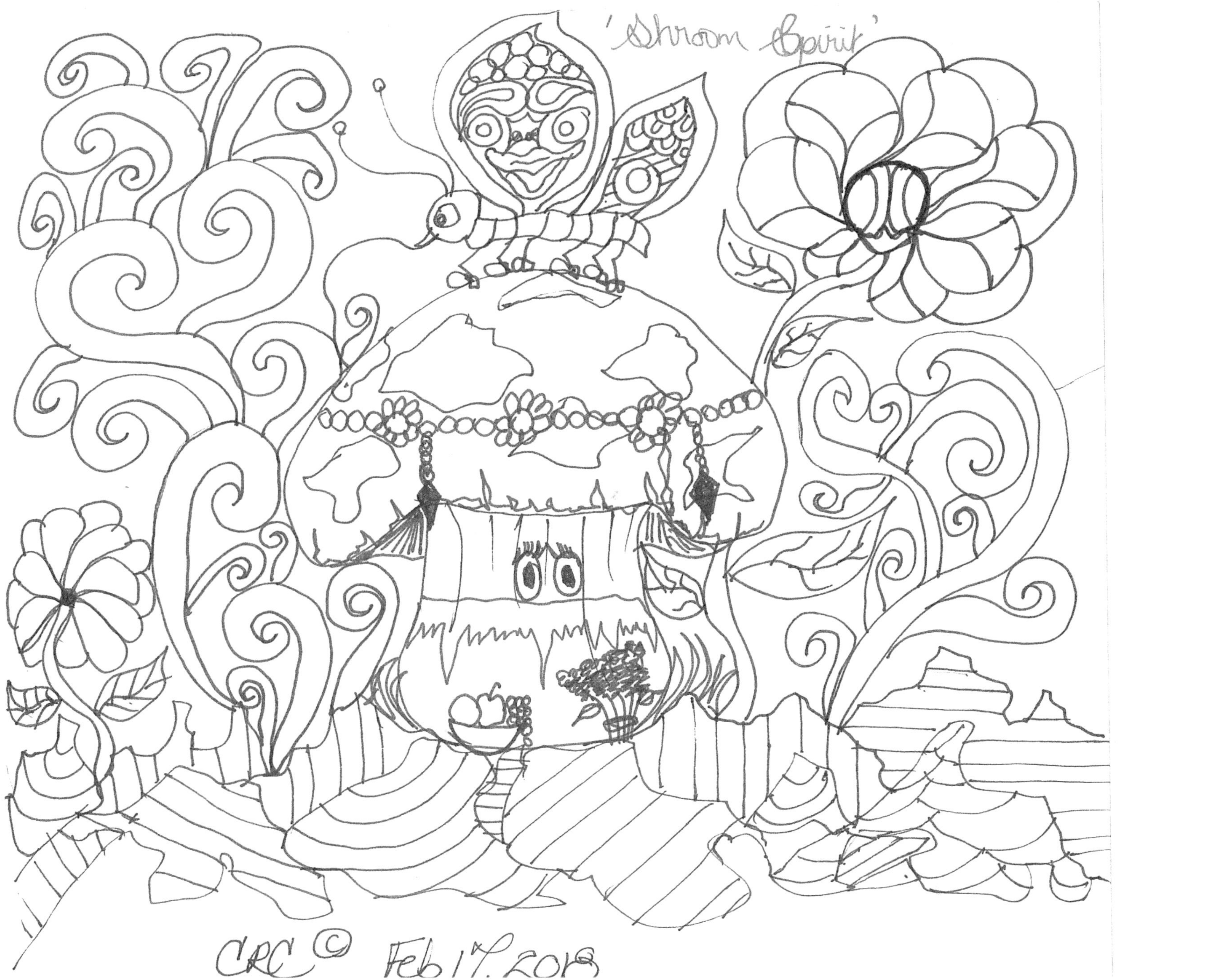
'Shroom Spirit'
CRC © Feb 17. 2018

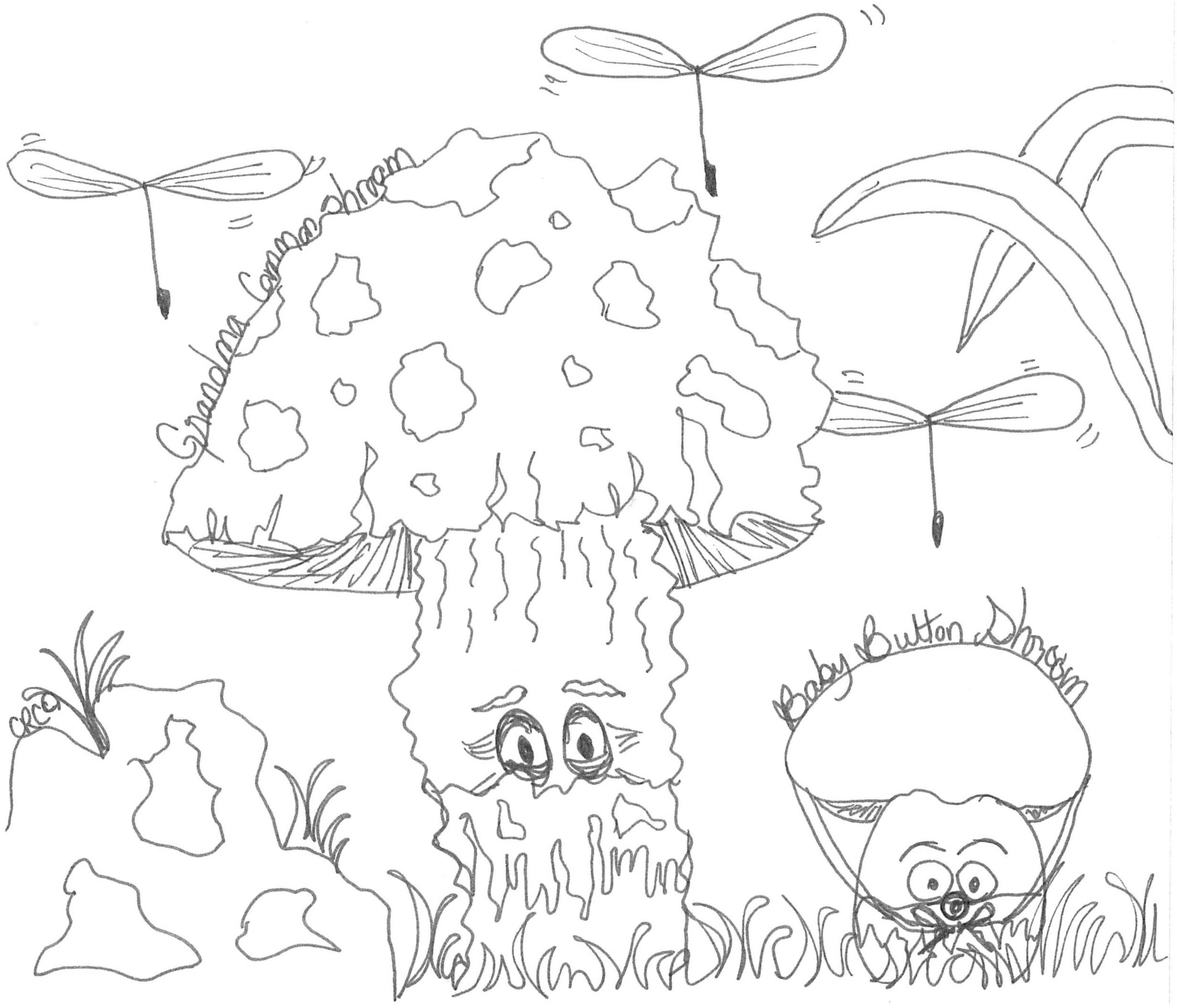
Grandma Common Shroom
Baby Button Shroom
CRC

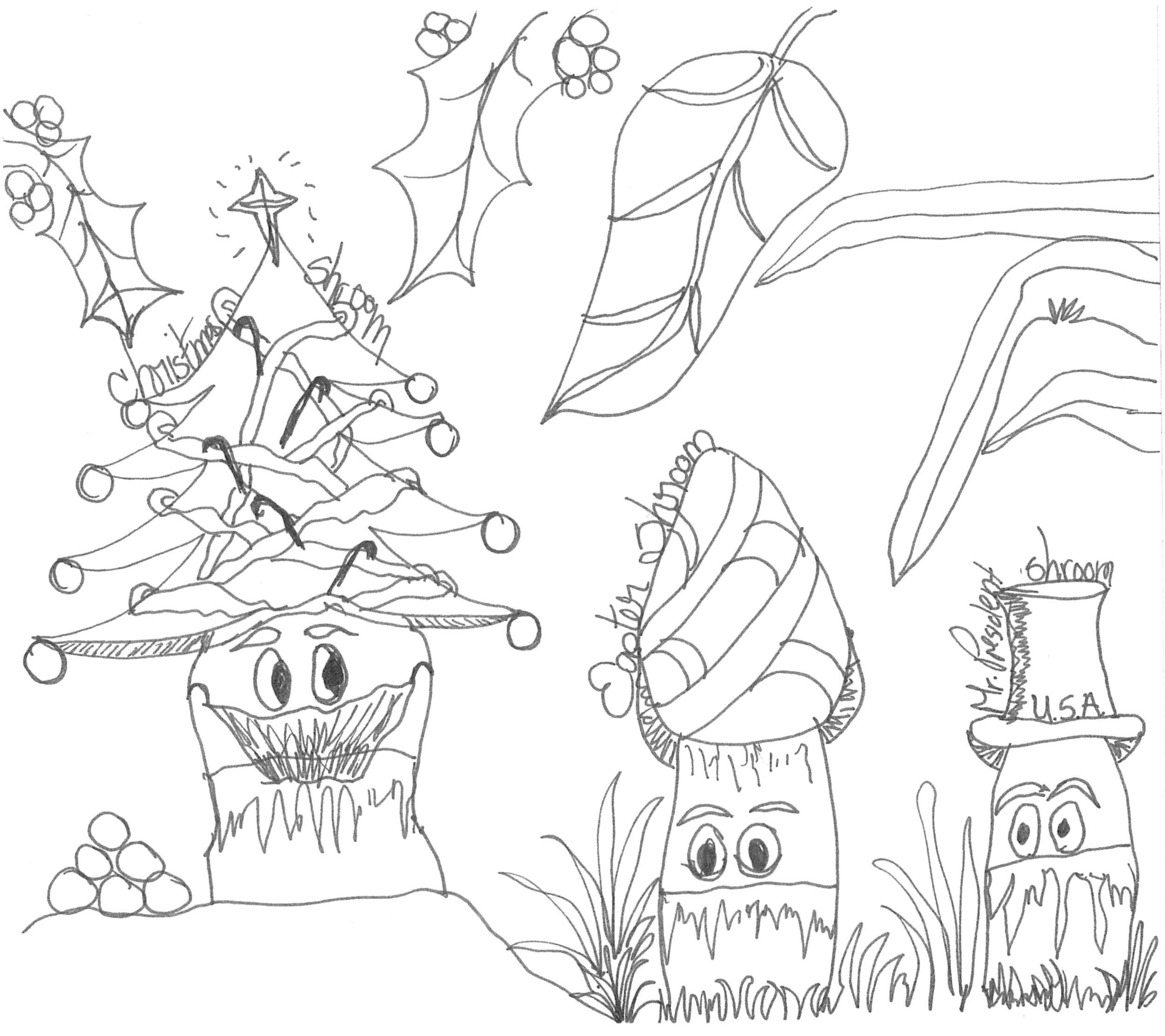
Christmas Shroom
Easter Shroom
Mr. President Shroom
U.S.A.

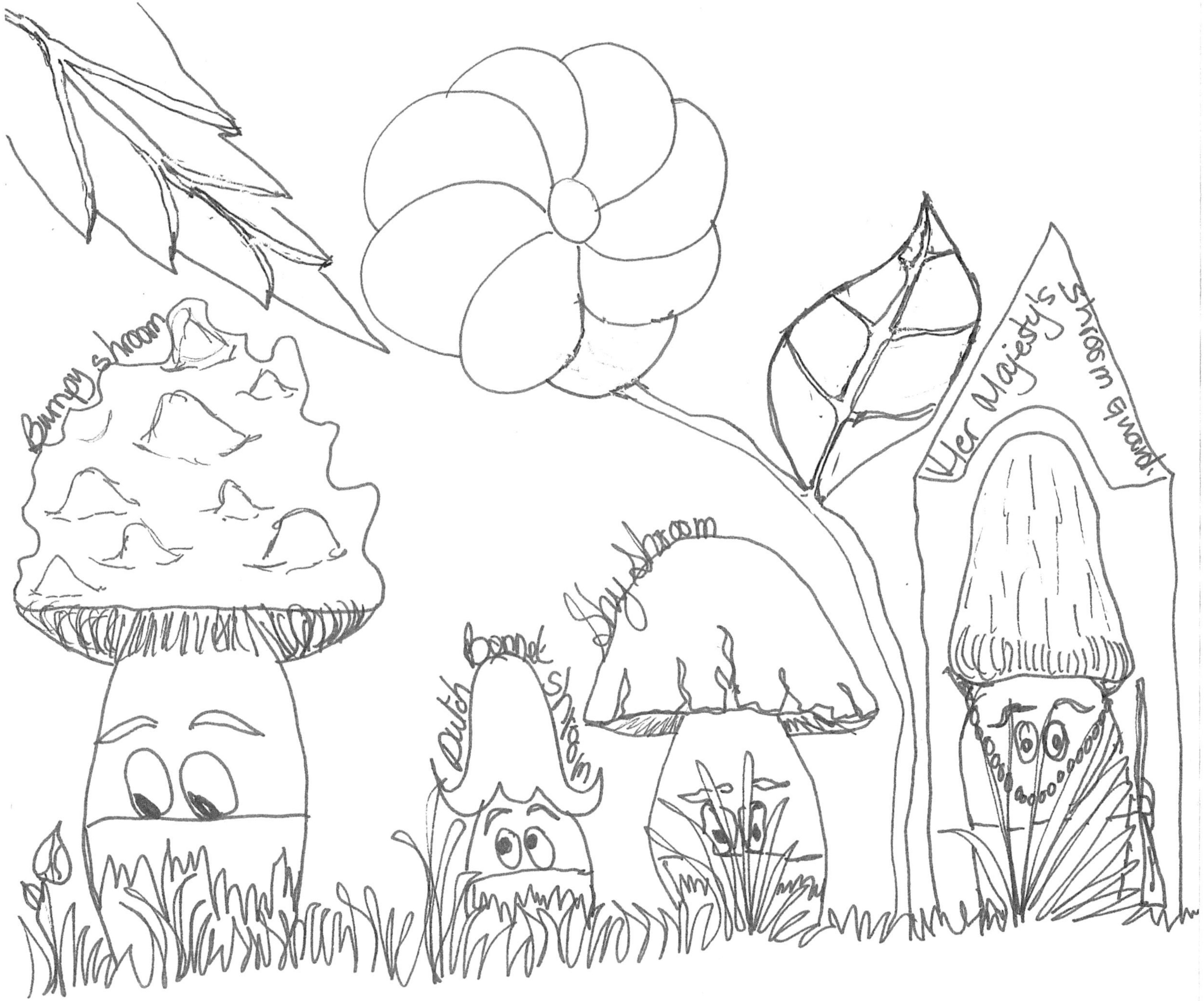
Bumpy shroom
Dutch bonnet shroom
Shy shroom
Her Majesty's shroom guard.

Name Those Shrooms!

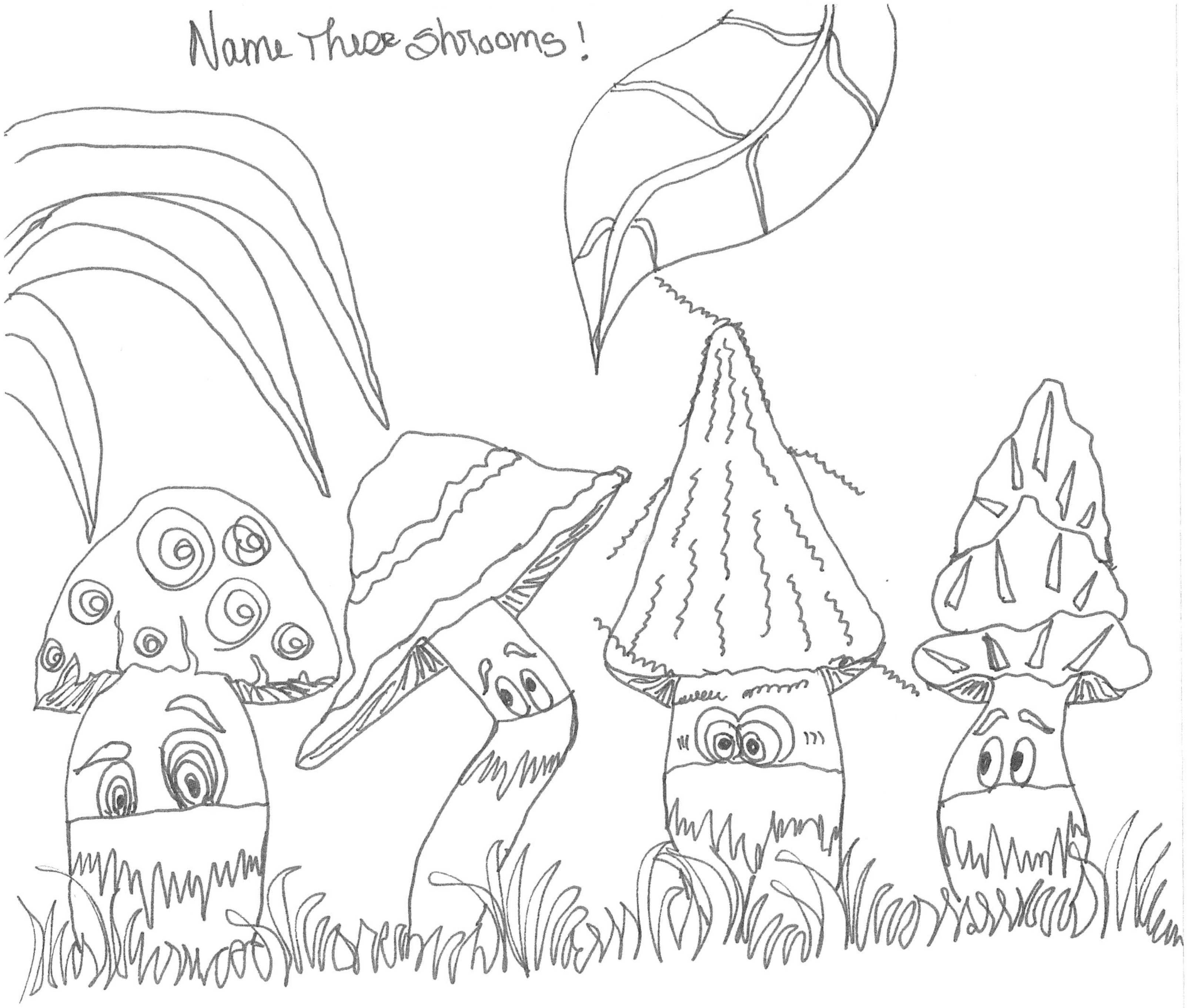

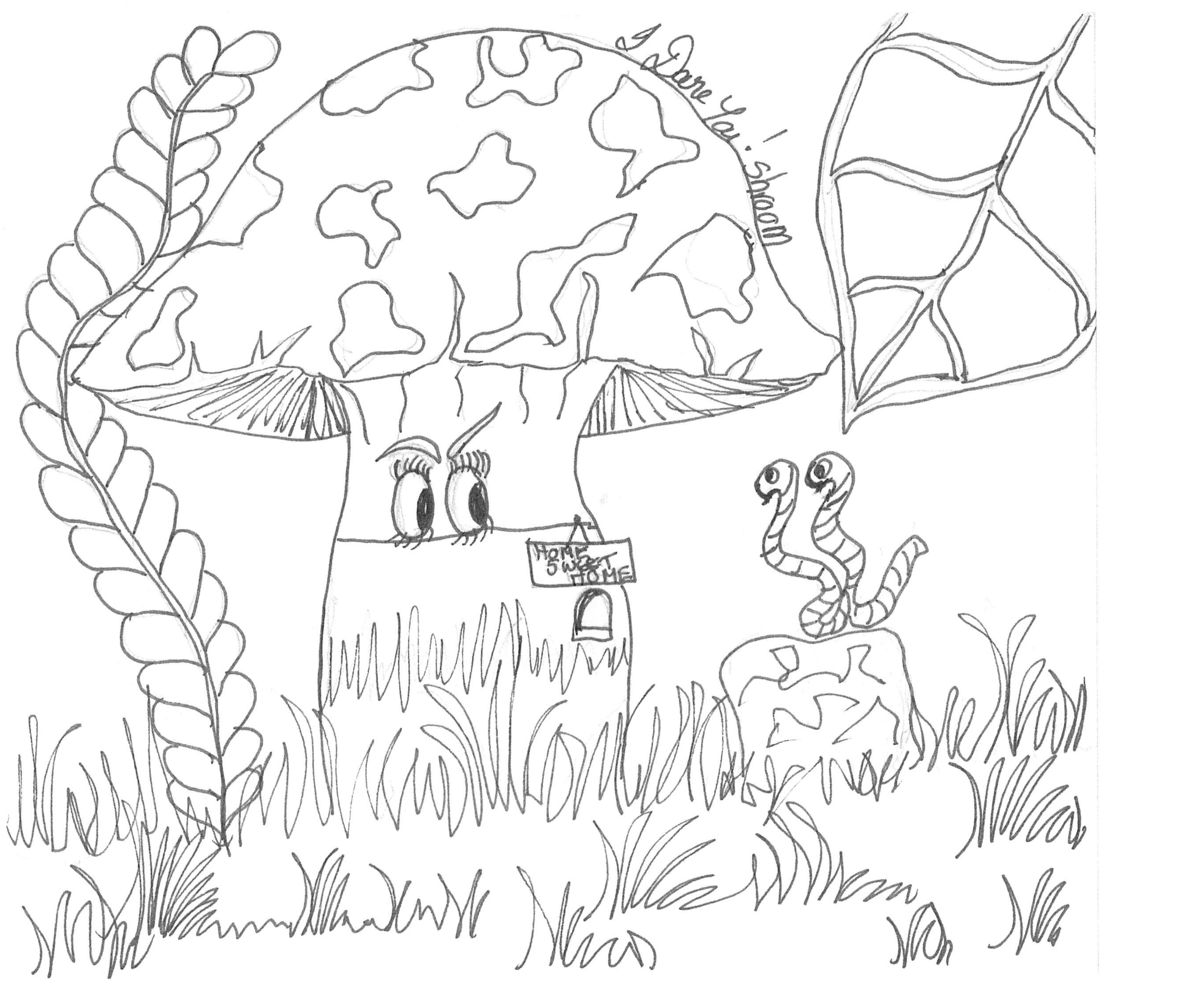
I Dare You! shroom
HOME SWEET HOME

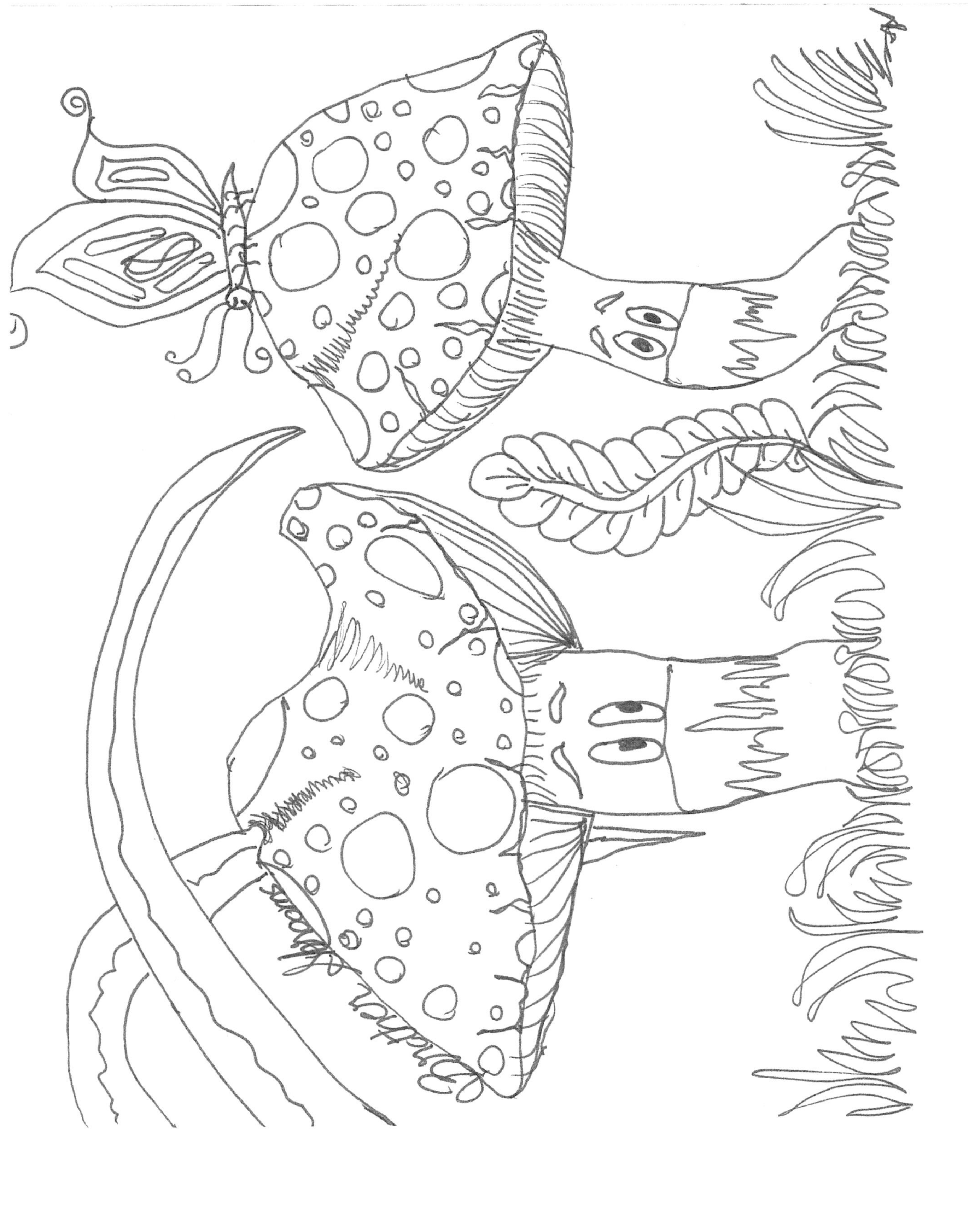

www.ingramcontent.com/pod-product-compliance
Lightning Source LLC
Chambersburg PA
CBHW080136240526
45468CB00009BA/2465
9781721253128